Jesus' Lonely Road

Devotional Guides
For Lent
And Holy Week

Robert C. Bankhead

CSS Publishing Company, Inc., Lima, Ohio

JESUS' LONELY ROAD

For more information about CSS Publishing Company resources, visit our website at
www.csspub.com.

ISBN 0-7880-1861-2   PRINTED IN U.S.A.

In memory of
Colonel Philip Burnes

In honor of
Mrs. Jo Burnes

Jesus' Lonely Road

Devotional Guide
For
Lent

Jesus' Lonely Road

Devotional Guide For Lent

Increasing Isolation from the Disciples,
    Growing Conflict with the Jewish Leaders.

A Lonely Journey

Mark 8:11-21, 31-33

Jesus walked that lonesome valley;
He had to walk it by himself;
'Cause nobody else could walk it for him;
He had to walk it by himself.

Jesus' journey to Jerusalem to be crucified was a lonely road. Jesus' relationship with the disciples was strained as they continually failed to understand his teaching. They challenged his predictions of impending death and his acceptance of children. They bickered among themselves over favored positions, and eventually they deserted him.

Conflict between Jesus and the Jewish leaders grew more personal as they challenged him over laws of the temple tax, of marriage and divorce, and his authority to teach. Jesus warned the disciples against the leaven of the Pharisees. His condemnation of the authorities reached a high point in the parables of the Two Sons and the Wicked Tenants, after which they intensified their efforts to arrest him. His denunciation peaked in a bitter pronouncement of a series of woes against the scribes, Pharisees, and hypocrites. Their animosity against Jesus culminated in a conspiracy to kill him.

The dual themes of isolation from the disciples and conflict with the Jewish leaders are joined in Jesus' first prediction of the Passion. He announced to the disciples that he must go to Jerusalem where he would suffer at the hands of the elders and chief priests and scribes, and be killed. Peter reacted vociferously, rebuking Jesus for such unacceptable thoughts. Jesus reprimanded Peter for his failure to understand and believe. From this moment on, the road to the cross grew more lonesome and stressful as Jesus walked the relentless pilgrimage that led to his death.

As you experience the season of Lent this year, read the narratives of Jesus' lonely road, and think of how you would have felt under the circumstances. Today, as you begin, think of how you would have responded when you heard Jesus announce he must suffer and die. Would you have tried to dissuade him, as Peter did? Consider how you would have felt if Jesus reprimanded you as harshly as he reprimanded Peter.

Are there not times in the church that we are hesitant to think about Jesus' suffering and death? We prefer positive themes of love and unity and peace. We like to think of Jesus as the precious child of Bethlehem, or the compassionate healer of the sick, or the glorified Lord ruling over all, rather than the crucified Lamb of God. Is not our reluctance to include the harsh themes of sacrifice and pain in our preaching and teaching a sign of our common agreement with Peter that these things should never have happened to Jesus?

For the rest of this week, read and meditate on Mark 8.

Thursday — Mark 8:22-26: Jesus' miracle of healing a blind man.
Friday — Mark 8:27-30: Jesus' retreat with the disciples to Caesarea Philippi.
Saturday — Mark 8:34—9:1: Jesus' exhortation to take up one's cross and follow.

> *I must walk that lonesome valley;*
> *I have to walk it by myself;*
> *'Cause nobody else can walk it for me;*
> *I have to walk it by myself.*

The Pilgrimage Begins

Mark 9:2-10, 30-37; 10:2-16

Jesus' pilgrimage to Jerusalem began on the Mount of Transfiguration, where he met with Moses and Elijah, symbolizing God's revelation in the Old Testament, through the Law and the Prophets. Jesus himself was the revelation of God's Incarnate Word in the New Testament. On the Mount the full revelation of the Word of God was gathered.

The inner circle of disciples, Peter, James, and John, who saw the vision of Jesus, transfigured in shining light, failed to understand this manifestation of God. They displayed their opposition to God's will when Peter suggested they build three tabernacles, one each for Moses, Elijah, and Jesus, and remain on the mountaintop. Perhaps he was thinking in this way to deter Jesus from the journey to Jerusalem and thus prevent Jesus' death.

When God spoke from heaven confirming that Jesus was God's Son, the Beloved, with whom God was well-pleased, the disciples again demonstrated their withdrawal, falling on the ground in fear, leaving Jesus alone until the vision was ended. When they came down from the mountain, Jesus solemnly instructed them not to tell anyone what they had seen, for he knew they would not understand until after the resurrection.

Jesus and the disciples set out from Galilee. Following the second prediction of the Passion, as they reached Capernaum, the disciples were bickering among themselves over greatness. Using a little child as his illustration Jesus taught them about humility and servanthood.

When they came to the region of Judea, a series of challenges by the Jewish authorities began. The Pharisees set out to test Jesus, challenging him over the laws of marriage and divorce. Recalling texts from Genesis 1:27 and 2:24, on the creation of humankind, Jesus refuted their argument from the Mosaic Law permitting divorce, and declared that any person who divorces a spouse, except

11

for the reason of unchastity, commits adultery. The Jewish leaders meekly submitted and made no further challenge at the moment. Their conflict with Jesus was still vague and unfocused.

Again the disciples failed to understand, and when they were alone with Jesus they asked him to explain. Next they challenged Jesus over his welcome acceptance of small children. Jesus instructed the disciples not to hinder him, declaring that the Kingdom of Heaven belonged to children such as these.

As you reflect on these passages, consider with whom you would have agreed. Would you have favored the Pharisee's obedience to the Law of Moses, or supported Jesus' unyielding denial of divorce? Would you have sided with the disciples over the distractions of children in church? Or would you have welcomed children even at the cost of dignity in the worship service?

This week read and meditate on Mark 9.

Monday — Mark 9:9-13: The role of the prophet, Elijah.

Tuesday — Mark 9:14-29: Jesus' miracle of healing an epileptic child.

Wednesday — Mark 9:33-37: Jesus' teaching on greatness and a child's example.

Thursday — Mark 9:38-41: Teaching on exorcism and compassionate service.

Friday — Mark 9:42-48: On stumbling blocks and deceiving oneself.

Saturday — Mark 9:49-50: The Parable of Salt.

Seeking Favoritism

Mark 10:32-45

Each time Jesus predicted his impending suffering and death, the band of disciples experienced a crisis. The third prediction of the Passion was followed by an ugly episode of two disciples seeking favored positions in Christ's kingdom, and the rest of the band reacting with anger and resentment.

Matthew and Mark report this episode as Jesus and the disciples were on the road to Jerusalem. This third prediction is the most detailed of the three. Jesus described his approaching ordeal in vivid terms, returning to an earlier theme in the first prediction that he would be handed over to the Jewish elders, chief priests, and scribes. They would condemn him to die, but lacking authority to execute him, they would hand him over to the Gentiles, who would mock and flog and spit upon him and kill him. The intensity of the three predictions of his death had reached its highest level.

Immediately following the prediction of the Passion is the account of two disciples' attempt to gain favor. Matthew and Mark differ in reporting who initiated the request. In Matthew, the mother of the sons of Zebedee made the request, and the sons were not specifically named. In Mark, James and John themselves asked to be allowed to sit on the right and left of Jesus in his coming glory. Sadly, Jesus asked if they were able to drink the cup of suffering he must drink. Mark adds, "Are you able to be baptized with the same baptism?" When they replied affirmatively that they were able, Jesus announced that he could not grant their request. It is for the Father in heaven to bestow this beneficence.

The result of this episode was disgruntlement and dissension among the band, for the other disciples were angry with James and John. Jesus used the crisis to teach a lesson on the quest for greatness and the meaning of servanthood. He taught them that the Son of Man came into the world not to be served, but to serve. Those who would be great must be servants of all.

13

As you reflect on these passages, think of our own attempts to gain power, or respect, or prestige over family, friends, and colleagues. How common it is for us to want to be first, even in the church. How often we think of ourselves more highly than is proper. How can we exercise the role of servant in our families, among our peers, with our fellow citizens? What does it mean to be a servant? Begin to list ways you might serve others in your community and in your church.

This week read and meditate on Mark 10.

Monday — Mark 10:13-16: Jesus' receiving the infant children.

Tuesday — Mark 10:17-22: Jesus' meeting with a rich young man.

Wednesday — Mark 10:23-27: Jesus' teaching on riches and heaven.

Thursday — Mark 10:28-31: Jesus' conversation with Peter, on discipleship.

Friday — Mark 10:35-40: A request by the sons of Zebedee.

Saturday — Mark 10:46-52: Jesus' miracle of healing a blind man, Bartimaeus.

The Conflict Intensifies

Mark 11:15-19, 27-32; 12:1-12

Jesus and the disciples reached Jerusalem where he began the final week of his life teaching daily in the Temple. We sense that the conflict was increasing and growing more personal. Jesus attacked the temple worship. The Jewish leaders challenged his authority to teach. Jesus responded with parables: 1) the Wicked Tenants, and 2) the Two Sons (only in Matthew 21:28-32). When the chief priests and Pharisees realized that Jesus was talking about them, they were furious and began to discuss ways they could arrest him.

Jesus had entered Jerusalem in triumph, with crowds singing praise and proclaiming him king. In the Temple he found a corrupt worship of commercial enterprise, changing money, and selling sacrificial animals for personal gain. Angry at the callous and greedy abuse of spiritual matters, Jesus turned over the tables of the merchants and drove them from the Temple. The chief priests and scribes were furious. They were so incensed they began to seek ways to destroy him, but they were afraid to do anything, for the crowds, who at the Triumphal Entry had proclaimed him king, eagerly approved his teaching.

Each evening Jesus left Jerusalem and walked back to Bethany to spend the night, probably with Simon the leper (Cf. Mark 14:3). Each morning he returned to the city and taught in the Temple. The chief priests and elders challenged his authority to teach. Jesus confronted them with a question over the baptism of John. Fearing the volatility of the crowds, they refused to answer and surrendered the debate to Jesus.

Jesus told two parables, which incited the Pharisees and chief priests. Mark records only the second, the Wicked Tenants. In the parable Jesus delivered his most scathing indictment of the leaders to date. Wicked tenants in a vineyard killed the owner's son to grab his inheritance. It was an unmistakable prediction of Jesus'

15

own death. The Pharisees and chief priests could not miss the point. Realizing that Jesus was talking about them, they secretly began to make plans to arrest him, but they were still afraid of his popularity with the crowds, and were frightened to take any open action.

In the other parable, found only in Matthew 21:28-32, Jesus told of two brothers, one who refused to do what his father requested, but then relented and did it; the second who agreed to do it, but never did. The story declared that publicans and prostitutes who believed in God would enter the Kingdom of Heaven before the Jewish leaders.

As you meditate on Jesus' parables, consider how church leaders, pastors, elders, and deacons may neglect, ignore, or even subvert the weightier matters of the gospel to protect and preserve the institutional church. Or consider how divisive issues between clergy and laity harm the true witness of the church. How often do we attack persons whose religious views and beliefs differ from our own, because we want to protect our interpretations? How seldom are we willing to listen with an open mind to someone else's defense of the faith?

This week read and meditate on Mark 11.

Monday — Mark 11:1-10: The Triumphal Entry.

Tuesday — Mark 11:15-18: Cleansing the Temple.

Wednesday — Mark 11:12-14, 20-24: A lesson from the barren fig tree.

Thursday — Mark 11:24-25: Jesus' teaching on prayer.

Friday — Mark 11:27-33: The Pharisees' challenge to Jesus' authority.

Saturday — Matthew 21:28-32: The Parable of the Two Sons.

A Series Of Challenges

Mark 12:13-37

As Jesus taught in the Temple, the Jewish authorities grew bolder, with a series of three challenges on the Law. First the Pharisees, then the Sadducees, then again the Pharisees took turns attacking Jesus, until Jesus turned and challenged them.

In the first challenge the Pharisees questioned Jesus about showing partiality, asking if it were lawful to pay taxes to Caesar. The growing conflict is evident in Mark's introduction of the question. He reports the Pharisees set out to entrap Jesus. Jesus recognized the tension. Aware of their malice, he called them hypocrites. Using his quick wit to turn their argument against them, he called for a coin, asking whose picture was stamped on it. When they answered it was the emperor's picture, he delivered the proverb, "Give to the emperor what belongs to the emperor, but give to God all that is God's." They meekly submitted and retired.

Next the Sadducees took their turn. Very conservative in their Jewish theology, they did not believe in resurrection, and asked Jesus a complex question of Jewish law. If a man died, having fathered no children, his brother was expected to marry his wife and assume family responsibility for her. The Sadducees posed a theoretical question, that if seven brothers in succession married a woman, whose wife would she be? Jesus was less patient with the Sadducees than with the Pharisees. He denounced their ignorance of scripture and of the ways of God. In the resurrection, marriage is not an issue. Because the crowds were astounded at his teaching, the Sadducees realized they had been beaten.

Again the Pharisees challenged him. Strict legalists concerning the Law, they hoped to catch Jesus in an injudicious statement. A lawyer asked him to select which law was the greatest. If he casually chose one law, they would accuse him of disparaging all the others. Jesus would not be trapped. He delivered the brilliant summary of the Law that has become the capstone of Christian

17

ethics. "Love the Lord your God with all your heart, and with all your soul, and with all your mind"; and "Love your neighbor as yourself."

Jesus then challenged the Pharisees with a question of faith in the Messiah, asking whose Son the Messiah was. When they answered, "the Son of David," he posed a rhetorical question of sonship and lordship. The Pharisees were duped, unable to answer, and stopped their attempts to trap Jesus. He had beaten them at their own game.

As you reflect on these challenges meditate on Jesus' Great Commandment. Review the Old Testament texts from which it comes — Deuteronomy 6:4-5 and Leviticus 19:18. How does it sum up the whole Law and the Prophets? What does it say for Christians as we begin the twenty-first century? How can we apply the commandment in the coming century? How does the commandment guide you in your own personal life?

This week read and meditate on Mark 12.

Monday — Mark 12:14-17: Jesus' teaching on taxes and support of the state.
Tuesday — Mark 12:18-27: Questions of resurrection and family relationships in heaven.
Wednesday — Mark 12:28-34: The Great Commandment.
Thursday — Mark 12:35-37: The Messiah and the Son of David.
Friday — Mark 12:38-40: Jesus' condemnation of the scribes.
Saturday — Mark 12:41-44: The example of the widow's mite.

Fifth Sunday In Lent

Pronouncing The Woes

Mark 12:38-40; see also Matthew 23:1-39

The culmination of Jesus' earlier warning against the leaven of the Pharisees and of Herod (Mark 8:14-21; Matthew 16:5-12) comes in Matthew with a series of scathing pronouncements of woe. There is an ironic twist. In the earlier passage, the disciples perceived that Jesus was warning them against the teaching of the Pharisees (Matthew 16:12); but in the latter passage (Matthew 23:2-3), Jesus instructed them to honor and respect the teaching of the scribes and Pharisees, for they were inheritors of the teaching of Moses. Jesus quickly cautioned the disciples to do what the Pharisees taught, not what they did. They acted adversely to what they said. Jesus accused the Pharisees of being hypocrites, teaching one thing, but doing something different. He used three illustrations of their hypocrisy: 1) putting heavy burdens of the Law upon their pupils but being unwilling to help them obey, 2) making ostentatious pretensions of righteousness, piety, and obedience, and 3) seeking places of prestige and honor.

Matthew collected a series of six woes that Jesus pronounced against the scribes and the Pharisees. Sharp, caustic denunciations, they show the animosity that had developed between Jesus and the Jewish leaders. Following the series of challenges the Pharisees and Sadducees made against Jesus in the preceding chapter (Mark 12; and Matthew 22), they demonstrate how intense and personal the conflict had become.

The six woes of which Jesus accused them were 1) self-righteous and insincere conversion of others, 2) unworthy use of oaths and expressions of faithfulness, 3) trivial misuse of tithing to avoid justice, mercy, and faith, 4) ostentatious application of the laws of purification, 5) outer appearance of righteousness but inner hypocrisy, and 6) pretentious honor of their ancestors while subverting the traditions. Jesus' animosity against the Jewish leaders was shown by his vitriolic denunciation, "You snakes! You brood of vipers! How can you escape being sentenced to hell?" (Matthew 23:33).

Of the six woes, the one most commonly quoted is the denunciation of their trivial tithing. Reflect on what Jesus was teaching about stewardship and the weightier matters of the Law. What does the passage say to you about tithing and stewardship? In Mark the short condemnation of the scribes (Mark 12:38-40) is followed by the example of the poor widow (Mark 12:41-44) who gave all she had. What does this add to our understanding of stewardship? How would you have felt if Jesus had denounced you as he denounced the Pharisees?

Relations between Jesus and the Pharisees had deteriorated to a bitter nadir. It leaves us with questions of tolerance for persons whose religious practices and beliefs differ from our own. How tolerant should we be when we disagree with other religions or other Christians who hold beliefs different from our faith?

This week meditate on Jesus' apocalyptic teaching, in Mark 13.

Monday — Mark 13:3-8: Signs of the Return of Christ.
Tuesday — Mark 13:9-13: Trials and Tribulation for the Faithful.
Wednesday — Mark 13:14-23: Suffering of the End Times.
Thursday — Mark 13:24-27: Appearance of the Son of Man.
Friday — Mark 13:28-31: Lesson of the Fig Tree.
Saturday — Mark 13:32-37: Watchful Waiting.

A Conspiracy To Kill

Mark 14:1-2, 10-50

In the liturgical calendar the last Sunday in Lent is recognized in one of two ways. First, as the conclusion of the Lenten Season, it is observed as the Sunday of the Passion, focusing our thought on the crucifixion and death of Jesus. Alternatively, as the first day of Holy Week, this Sunday is known as Palm Sunday, commemorating Jesus' Triumphal Entry into Jerusalem. This devotional guide follows the first tradition.

The culmination of Jesus' lonely road unfolded as his conflict with the Jewish authorities resulted in a conspiracy to arrest and destroy him. Judas betrayed him. Jesus predicted Peter would deny him, and the disciples all deserted him.

Again, as Jesus made plans for the observance of the Passover, he predicted his death by crucifixion. The chief priests and elders began making plans to arrest and kill him. They conspired to find a way to destroy him. Still afraid of the crowds and fearing the mob might turn into a riot, they discussed ways to arrest him in secret. A stroke of evil luck fell their way. Judas Iscariot, one of the twelve disciples, for whatever reason disillusioned and despondent, turned against Jesus and decided to betray him, offering to sell Jesus out to the chief priests for money. The conspiracy was sealed. The Jewish authorities had their means of arresting and destroying Jesus.

When Jesus gathered the twelve for the Passover meal, he played a charade with them to announce that one of them would betray him. They were all astonished and began asking, "Surely not I, Lord?" He responded that it was one who dipped his hand in the bowl with him, as they all had done.

Jesus predicted all the disciples would desert him. Peter vociferously objected, professing his loyalty even to death, to which Jesus responded by predicting Peter would deny him. Retiring to the Garden of Gethsemane to pray, Jesus took Peter, James, and

John to support him as he prepared for the ordeal he must face. Symbolically they deserted him by falling asleep as he prayed for God to deliver him.

When he had finished praying, as they were leaving the garden, Judas appeared with a vigilante mob from the chief priests and elders, and betrayed Jesus with a kiss, just as Jesus had predicted. The Pharisees' conspiracy to destroy Jesus had succeeded. He had been handed over to the Jewish authorities, just as he had often predicted. In fear, the disciples all fled, abandoning Jesus, just as he had predicted. Jesus was left, all alone, to face the ordeal of the Passion.

For your personal reflection on this day you are encouraged to consider with whom you might have stood. With Judas — Why did Judas betray him? With Peter — Why did Peter deny him? With the disciples — Why did they desert him? Why did Jesus have to stand all alone?

Jesus walked that lonesome valley;
He had to walk it by himself;
'Cause nobody else could walk it for him;
He had to walk it by himself.

Coronation
To
Crucifixion

Devotional Guide
For
Holy Week

Coronation To Crucifixion
Shadows Of The Cross

Devotional Guide For Holy Week

The Way of the Cross takes Jesus
From a Triumphal Entry to Death at Calvary

The Crowds Proclaimed Him King

Mark 11:1-11

Though surrounded by crowds of people who ran along the roadside calling him King of the Jews, Jesus rode alone into the city of Jerusalem. Only he knew the ordeal he must face. Only he knew the suffering and pain and death that awaited him. Only he knew what must take place before the week was ended. He came to the holy city in solitary majesty, alone in the midst of shouting multitudes.

The Triumphal Entry into Jerusalem is marked by startling contradictions. Jesus rode in regal splendor, as a king riding to his coronation. Yet amid the sights and sounds of a royal court, he sat meek and lowly, a humble monarch. A royal path covered by branches stripped from the trees and bushes lining the roadway formed a lush carpet of green. Yet the road he must walk before the Sabbath led not to a throne, but to a cross. The crowds followed along the way, singing and shouting and rejoicing, ready to crown him king. But quiet and sedate he sat amid the clamor of their voices, his countenance sad and pensive. He knew that the same multitudes who sang his praise would by week's end shout in anger and hatred, and demand his death. Those who joined his procession into the city, rejoicing and singing, would accompany the death squad to Golgotha, laughing at him and taunting him as he hung on the cross. Those ready to seat him on a throne would demand he be nailed to a cross. On the road into the city, the coronation parade passed by the Mount of Olives, where five days later he would pray earnestly for God to deliver him. He sat on a colt provided for him to ride in majesty, but he would retrace the road to Calvary with a stranger forced to carry his cross. By the end of the week he would travel the road from coronation to crucifixion. Triumph would turn to despair. He would go from sovereign king to suffering servant.

As you begin the way of the cross with Jesus this Holy Week, imagine yourself among the crowds lining the roadway, singing his praise. Would you have felt the exhilarating joy of the moment? Or would you have seen the sorrow in Jesus' eyes? Would you have joined the crowd proclaiming him king, expecting him to gather an army and lead it into battle to deliver your people from the oppression of hated enemies? Or would you have recognized the demeanor of a humble, lowly king? Would you have thought him to be the one you had been expecting? Or would you have felt betrayed because he was not the one you were waiting for?

Through this week, travel with Jesus along the road to the cross. Listen to him as he taught in the Temple. Watch reverently as his body was anointed for his death by an unknown woman. Feel with him the disappointment and sorrow of betrayal, denial, and desertion. Share with him a Last Supper, and pray with him an anguished prayer in the garden. Then stand at the foot of the cross as he died for your salvation, and confess your faith, "Surely this was the Son of God."

Monday Of Holy Week

Jesus Taught In The Temple

Mark 11:27—12:12

Each evening through the first days of his last week, Jesus walked from the holy city, Jerusalem, to the village of Bethany, to spend the night, to rest and sleep, to renew his strength, and to prepare for his ordeal. Each morning he returned to Jerusalem, where he spent the day teaching in the Temple. The crowds gathered to hear him, astonished with his wisdom. They listened intently. He taught with authority and understanding.

The Pharisees and Jewish leaders challenged him, but he answered every objection wisely, interpreting the Jewish Law with teaching so plain and simple that everyone could understand. He gave them the great commandment. He taught them about social customs and about stewardship and sacrificial giving.

He taught with parables. In one parable he spoke of a landowner who planted a vineyard, building a fence surrounding it to protect it, hewing out a winepress and erecting a watchtower. Perhaps Jesus was thinking of Isaiah's parable of the vineyard (Isaiah 5:1-7). When it was necessary for the owner to journey to another country, he contracted with sharecroppers to tend the vineyard. At harvest time, expecting to share in the profits, the owner sent a servant to collect his due. But the tenants attacked and beat up the slave. The owner sent a second servant, who was also beaten, and a third servant, whom the tenants killed. Finally, the owner sent his beloved son, but again the sharecroppers killed the son, hoping to claim the inheritance.

The meaning of the parable was clear. God had lavished tender care on a chosen people, entrusting them to the compassion of religious leaders. God had sent them lawgivers, teachers, priests, and prophets, but the religious leaders had abused God's messengers and misled God's people. God had expected the keepers of the chosen people to bring rich fruits of spiritual leadership, but they had returned only hypocrisy and misdirection. Finally, God had sent God's own beloved son, but the religious leaders were preparing to kill him. The parable predicted that God would take the people from the religious leaders.

The parable clearly anticipated Jesus' death, which was rapidly drawing near. Here, in the Temple, at the beginning of the week, Jesus described in a frightening manner his own death a few short days later. His teaching was delivered under the shadow of the cross.

In your meditation today, imagine that you were in the Temple listening to Jesus. How would you have felt? Would you have understood his poignant prediction of death? Would you have tried to dissuade him? Would you have believed his solemn warning? Would you have felt sympathy for the religious leaders, who perceived a threat to their comfortable faith?

Tuesday Of Holy Week

A Woman Anointed Jesus' Head

Mark 14:3-9

She was a face in the shadows, a nameless woman who slipped into the room where Jesus sat with friends, eating the evening meal, relaxing after the long day of teaching in the Temple. The Gospel writer tells us that it was in the home of Simon the leper, but didn't consider it important to tell us her name. Simon's guests scarcely noticed that she had come in, off the street, until she stepped up behind Jesus and poured an alabaster jar of expensive nard on his head. The diners were shocked. It happened so quickly they were caught off guard and embarrassed. They began to gripe and complain. They accused her of wasting the precious ointment. It was very valuable. Someone suggested it was worth 300 denarii. Someone else thought it might have been sold and the money given to the poor. They began to scold her.

Jesus reacted just the opposite. He rebuked the disciples for their insensitivity and lack of understanding. She had performed a valuable gesture of respect and honor, for which Jesus was profoundly appreciative. What had she done? Jesus realized that she had anointed his body for his burial. It was a powerful anticipation of his impending death. Perhaps Jesus knew that after his crucifixion there would not be enough time to prepare the body properly for burial, before the beginning of the Sabbath. She had done symbolically what the women would be unable to do before his body was placed in the tomb.

As Jesus moved through this last week, the counterpoint of adoration in contrast to Jesus' death by crucifixion drives the narrative. She came from the unknown crowds to honor him. But her thoughtful act was hidden in the shadow of the cross. Her caring gesture pointed unmistakably to his impending death.

If you had been at the table that night, how would you have responded? Would you have felt the wasteful gesture was callous?

31

After all, the money could have relieved the suffering from poverty for a number of people. Would you have felt Jesus was a bit insensitive in commenting on the poor as always present? Or would you have recognized the sensitive gift for the Son of God? What common arguments in churches can you remember over the use of benevolences, or capital building funds, and local congregational expenses? Is it insensitive to spend money for current expenses or to build new sanctuaries for ourselves rather than a soup kitchen to feed the poor? How can a congregation act responsibly in its stewardship to the many needs of both congregation and others?

Friends Gathered For A Sacred Meal

Mark 14:10-31

Jesus' last supper with the twelve disciples was an occasion of high tension and mixed emotions. First, Judas Iscariot decided he could no longer support Jesus and began making plans to betray him. He went to the Jewish leaders and offered to turn Jesus over to them if they paid him. They were ecstatic and quickly agreed. Judas started looking for a time to deliver Jesus into their hands. It was the first serious defection from the band of friends who had been so close to Jesus throughout his ministry. When Jesus announced at the supper that one of the twelve would betray him, it marked a turning point for the chosen disciples. The initial twelve would never again be together. One disciple had turned away.

In strong contrast to the pathos of betrayal, there was the solemn observance of the holiest of the holy Jewish festivals. It recalled the night of Exodus from Egypt when the angel of death passed over the houses of the Israelites because the blood of an innocent lamb was smeared on the lintels of the gates. By the mighty hand of God the Israelites were set free from their bondage, delivered from slavery, and set on their journey to the promised land. Each year the people of Israel gathered for Passover. It was this festival Jesus and the disciples gathered in the Upper Room to celebrate. It was a joyous and moving occasion, observed with solemn and deep-felt thanksgiving. Dominating the occasion, however, was the shadow of the cross and the tension of Jesus' shocking announcement of betrayal. The disciples, distressed and confused, began asking one by one, "Surely, not I?"

In distributing the bread and wine of the Passover meal, Jesus foreshadowed his sacrificial death. Breaking the bread, he solemnly declared, "This is my body." Passing the cup, he proclaimed, "This is my blood of the new covenant, which is poured out for many." The profound meaning of the occasion was overshadowed by his impending death. The joy of the occasion was muted with sorrow and apprehension.

As they left the room after the meal, Jesus made two further predictions which increased the tension among the band of disciples and led to their vehement denial. First, he announced that all the disciples would desert him, leaving him to face the ordeal of the Passion alone. Simon Peter, the strong, impetuous fisherman who had become the leader of the group, was offended, and declared angrily that although the others might desert Jesus, he would remain faithful, even if it meant his death. Sadly, Jesus predicted that Peter would deny he even knew Jesus three times before the rooster crowed to foretell the dawn. With clamorous protestations of loyalty from all the disciples, the band, now feeling the tension and torn apart with dissension, left the Upper Room and went into the dark, sinister night.

Can you imagine yourself in the Upper Room, celebrating Passover with Jesus? Do you understand why Judas Iscariot agreed to betray him? Was he disappointed over Jesus' unwillingness to fight the hated Romans? Was he angry because he thought Jesus had misled them? Was he hoping to shock Jesus into action? Was he discouraged because Jesus was not the one he was hoping for? How would you have felt if Jesus predicted you would desert him? Would you have understood the disciples' fear? Would you have tried to persuade Jesus to flee before the Jewish authorities could arrest him?

Maundy Thursday

Jesus Prayed In The Garden

Mark 14:32-50

From the Upper Room into the dark night Jesus led the disciples to a private, secluded spot in the Garden of Gethsemane. Asking the band, now eleven, to sit and wait for him, he took the inner circle, Peter, James, and John, a bit further and asked them to watch for him, so that he would not be disturbed as he prepared himself for the coming ordeal. Knowing what he must face, he did not want to begin until he had spent time with God, his Father. Well did he know the spiritual strength of quiet prayer and devotion. Often throughout his ministry he had withdrawn from the busy crowds to pray when there was an important decision to be made or a difficult task to be accomplished. He had found in quiet moments with God the guidance and strength and aid he needed.

We should not pass lightly by the ominous clouds hanging over his death. It was no routine prayer that Jesus intoned. His heart was heavy; his spirit anguished. He shared his agony with the disciples, telling them that he was deeply distressed. To God he confessed his fear, begging God that if there were any way possible that he be spared the Passion. It was an honest prayer. He earnestly wished he did not have to suffer and die. Even though he had known his ministry must come to this, even though he had come to Jerusalem expecting to die, he made one final appeal for God to spare him.

The prayer, however, was a devotional discipline of perfect submission to the will of God. Even as he prayed to be delivered, he declared his obedience. He prayed most fervently, "Not what I wish, but your will, O Father." He was the obedient Son, fully willing to finish what God had sent him to do, to complete what he had come into the world to accomplish.

Jesus' devotion is a contrast to the disciples' abandonment. Tired and sleepy from the long day, realizing they would not return to Bethany to rest this night, they settled down, got comfortable, and fell asleep. This anticipated the desertion Jesus had predicted and their flight at his arrest. In the garden Jesus was alone in his prayers.

In the garden, secluded from the crowds who had supported Jesus, Judas found the opportunity he had been looking for to betray Jesus. Judas, realizing that Jesus would go to the garden to pray, had gone to find the Jewish leaders, the chief priests and scribes and elders, who had agreed to pay Judas for leading them to Jesus at a time they could arrest him. He led them to the garden, and as he had promised, he kissed Jesus to identify him to the mob. Jesus submitted willingly, and the disciples ran away in fear. The ordeal of the Passion had begun.

As you reflect on Jesus' prayer in the garden, think of occasions in your own life when you have found spiritual strength in moments of prayer and devotion. Withdrawal into the quiet discipline of prayer prepares us for difficult times. Brief moments of devotion spent in the presence of God give us strength and guidance and help for living through the day. They are times to be treasured in our spiritual pilgrimage. We have not faced the ordeal Jesus endured, but just as he found spiritual strength, we also are strengthened in prayer.

The Crowds Demanded Jesus' Death

Mark 15:1-39

Early in the morning, as soon as the first rays of the sun began to appear, the Jewish council turned Jesus over to Pontius Pilate, the Roman governor. The Sanhedrin had examined him through the long night and they were determined that he be executed. It was quite early, since the trial before Pilate, the preparations for crucifixion, and the trek to Calvary were completed before 9 a.m. Jesus was nailed to the cross by the third hour of the day (9 a.m.).

Pilate was convinced that Jesus was innocent of the charges brought against him. He realized that the chief priests had condemned Jesus out of spite and jealousy. Pilate tried to find a way to set Jesus free. There was a custom that allowed him to declare amnesty for one prisoner during the festival. Pilate proposed that he release Jesus. But the chief priests, working the mob, stirred up the crowd to demand another prisoner, Barabbas. Barabbas was a murderer who had been arrested in an attempted rebellion. When Pilate asked what they wanted him to do with Jesus, they shouted, "Crucify him!" Pilate, afraid of a riot, and wanting to appease the mob, sentenced Jesus to die.

It was an unruly, boisterous crowd, goaded on by the chief priests, and incited by the false accusations, hyperemotional over the festival. The mob fed on its own excitement, becoming more and more uncontrollable, wandering through the streets, standing outside the Praetorian, shouting and demanding Jesus' death. It was a classic example of mob psychology dominating the crowd and inciting a riot.

These were the same people who five days earlier had followed Jesus in triumph into the city, singing his praise, ready to crown him their king. They were the same multitudes who gathered each day at the Temple, listening intently, astonished and amazed at his wisdom and authority. They were the ones whom the Jewish authorities feared because they believed Jesus to be a prophet. So quickly they had turned against him. They demanded his death, and Pilate granted it.

One further scene illustrates the crowd's angry, rebellious spirit against Jesus. They followed the execution squad along the road, retracing the steps they had walked during the Triumphal Entry. Again it was a festive procession. On the way to watch an execution, they were being entertained, shouting and laughing and making ribald jokes. They jeered at Jesus and taunted him when he was too weak to carry his own cross, and Simon of Cyrene was jerked out of the crowd and forced to carry it. Arriving at the mount of crucifixion they watched as the soldiers nailed Jesus to the cross. Then they sat down to watch him die. They dared him to come down from the cross. Crowds of pilgrims passing by joined in the mocking derision. The chief priests and the scribes moved among the mob, continuing to mock him, inciting their anger and hate. Amid the macabre scene, Jesus died. The road from coronation to crucifixion had come to its inevitable end.

If you had been in the crowd, would you have been able to dissuade Pilate from sentencing Jesus to death? Would you have tried to turn the crowd's fierce anger away from Jesus? Would you have resisted the Jewish authorities seeking Jesus' death? Imagine yourself caught in the swelling tide of mob violence. How would you have tried to defend Jesus?

The Women Waited

Mark 15:40-47

The gospel writers have a profound appreciation for the ministrations of women in service to the crucified Jesus. The narrative of Jesus' burial is bracketed by notices that the women were present watching over the closing moments of Jesus' life. At the crucifixion were Mary Magdalene, Mary, the mother of Joses, and other women who had come with him to Jerusalem. They had cared for him and provided for him in Galilee.

When Jesus died around 3 p.m., the time was too short to prepare the body properly for burial before the beginning of Sabbath at 6 p.m. Joseph of Arimathea, a member of the Council, but a follower of Jesus, asked Pilate for permission to take the body and bury it. Discerning that Jesus was dead, Pilate consented. Joseph wrapped the body in a linen cloth and laid it in a tomb hewn out of rock.

Following the body to the grave, watching where it was placed, were the women, Mary Magdalene and the other Mary. They were making plans to return to the tomb once the Sabbath was over to anoint the body with spices and complete the proper burial ritual. It was these women who came very early on Easter morning, carrying the spices. It was they who were the first witnesses of the glorious resurrection. They had ministered to Jesus in his ministry; they had been loyal, standing by him in his death. They were the first to hear the good news that he was risen from the dead.

The day Jesus' body lay in the tomb has come to be known as the Great Vigil. It is a day of meditation and prayer, remembering Jesus' passion and preparing to celebrate the wondrous miracle of resurrection. In your devotionals you are encouraged to prepare yourself for the Good News of Easter with a day of Bible reading, meditation, and prayer. It is suggested that through the day you read the Lectionary passages for the Day of the Easter Vigil.

The Old Testament Readings
Genesis 1:1—2:4a
Genesis 7:1-5, 11-18; 8:6-18; 9:8-13
Genesis 22:1-18
Exodus 14:10-31; 15:20-21
Isaiah 55:1-11
Proverbs 8:1-8, 19-21; 9:4b-6
Ezekiel 36:24-28
Ezekiel 37:1-14
Zephaniah 3:14-20

The Psalter Readings
Psalm 136:1-9, 23-26
Psalm 46
Psalm 16
Exodus 15:1b-13, 17-18
Isaiah 12:2-6
Psalm 19
Psalms 42 and 43
Psalm 143
Psalm 98

The New Testament Reading
Romans 6:3-11

Psalm 114

The Gospel Reading
Mark 16:1-8